W9-BTL-582

To Uju Darko and Chizuba for making this book possible

JANETTA OTTER-BARRY BOOKS

While the events portrayed in *Vicky Goes to the Doctor* are authentic,
this book is a work of fiction and may not resemble a real-life situation.

Vicky Goes to the Doctor copyright © Frances Lincoln Limited 2013
Text and photographs copyright © Ifeoma Onyefulu 2013

First published in Great Britain in 2013 and in the USA in 2014 by
Frances Lincoln Children's Books, 4 Torriano Mews,
Torriano Avenue, London NW5 2RZ
www.franceslincoln.com

All rights reserved

No part of this publication may be reproduced, stored in a retrieval system,
or transmitted, in any form, or by any means, electrical, mechanical, photocopying,
recording or otherwise without the prior written permission of the publisher or a licence permitting
restricted copying. In the United Kingdom such licences are issued by the Copyright Licensing Agency,
Saffron House, 6-10 Kirby Street, London EC1N 8TS.

A catalogue record for this book is available from the British Library.

ISBN 978-1-84780-363-4

Set in Green

Printed in Shenzhen, Guangdong, China by CGC Offset Printing in May, 2013.

135798642

VICKY GOES TO THE DOCTOR

Ifeoma Onyefulu

FRANCES LINCOLN
CHILDREN'S BOOKS

This is Vicky.

Vicky loves playing and running around,
but today she's very quiet.

She won't eat her mother's food,

or play with her friends,

or do any drawings.

What is the matter with Vicky?
Her father feels her forehead.
"Vicky's head is hot," he says.
"She's not well."

Oh, poor Vicky!

"Child, I'm taking you to see the doctor,"
says her mother, and she quickly
helps Vicky get dressed.

Later, they stand by the side of the road, waiting for a taxi.

Where are all the taxis when you need one?

Luckily the clinic isn't too far away,
so they walk.

They're nearly there. . . .

Here they are, waiting to see
the doctor.

At last, the doctor is ready to see them.

"Hello," she smiles. "What is the matter, child?"

"Vicky is not well," says her mother.

Vicky is a little scared, but her mother
gives her a big hug.

The doctor takes Vicky's temperature
and listens to her chest.

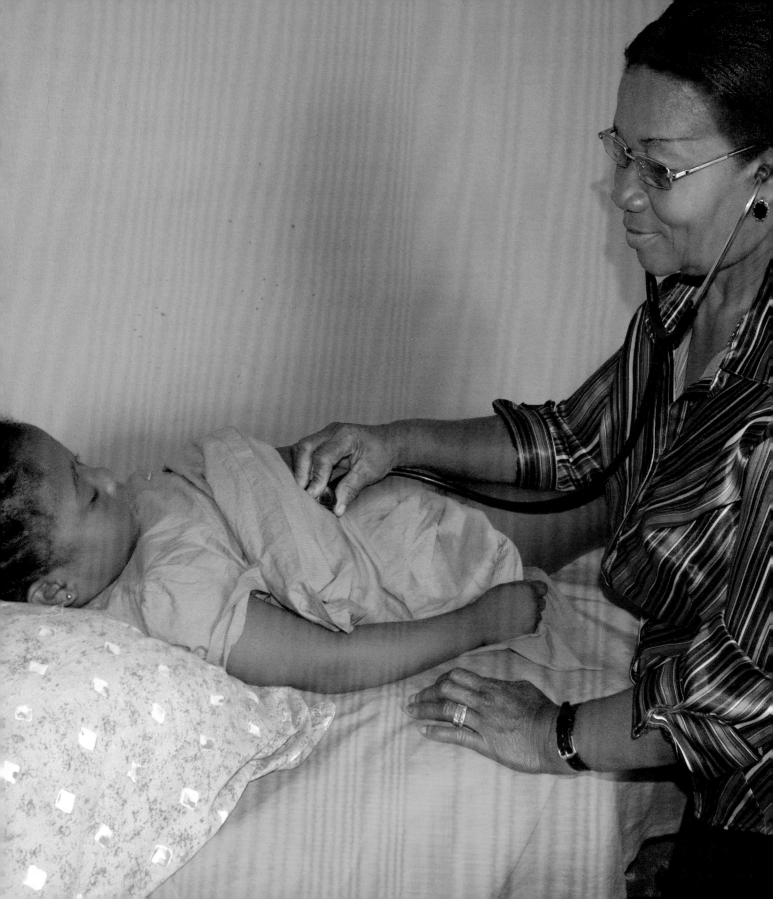

"Keep her cool, Madam,"
says the doctor, "and give
her lots of water.
If she's not better by
tomorrow, come back
and see me, please."

Later, Vicky is feeling much better.

And thankfully she's eating again,

drawing pictures,

and playing with
her friends!